Lauren —
Your book looks &
reads very well! Hope you
enjoy this — it's the real
me. Charlie Haden
2015

THE ART of LIFE

Observations on American Life

commentary & artworks by **Charles J. Hamm**

◄ *Sun Room*, Oil and acrylic on canvas, 24"x18"

The Art of Life: Observations on American Life

©2015 Charles J. Hamm

ISBN 13: 978-1-63381-033-4

photography of artwork by John Urgo

designed and produced by
Maine Authors Publishing
558 Main Street, Rockland, Maine 04841
www.maineauthorspublishing.com

Manufactured in the United States of America

For Irene, Charles and Liza…each helped me develop.

CONTENTS

◄ *Relationships #1*, Oil and acrylic on canvas, 24"x18"

Introduction

MY FATHER—MAYBE EVERYONE'S FATHER—THOUGHT each of us had a book in them. After 77 years, this is my book. I invite you to discover the book within *you*.

My early years (and many later) were tough. I could not read or write very well. Lousy student. Learning disabilities. I thought I was sort of dumb. So I listened a lot. Laid back. Waited for learning.

Noticed people *talked* more than understood or taught. People seemed to become frustrated finding the essence of things, central ideas. Lots of people thought others were not listening to them if there were disagreements. "You're not listening to me!" as opposed to "Do you understand?" or "Why don't you agree?" Most of the time, too many words got in the way. How about "I'm not being clear, am I?"

For most of my life, I have needed to pursue the essence of thoughts. Partly not to waste time. Partly to create understandings. That's what I hope this is about. The art of life. Oversimplified but I hope central. Certainly controversial.

◀ *First Life*, Acrylic on board, 36"x24"

Essence

LET'S SIMPLIFY. I FIND PEOPLE NEED TO BE understood, appreciated, and correct. In order to do this, they need to be able to have a good conversation at cocktail parties. An opinion I have developed is that most good discussions should begin when you have a core understanding of your own beliefs. To help here, begin with the fundamentals. Ideas and points of view may be initially parsed into halves. For example, some halves are clearly simple—up/down, black/white, yes/no—you get the idea.

My first insight into halvings occurred early in my career in advertising. We were testing how far we could go in researching toilet tissue. The big finding was that half of the U.S. population were folders and half were crumplers. Simple, right?

Other halves are more complex. For example: truth/ fact, emotion/reason, take/give. How about God/god? *God* referring to formal religion; *god* being the idea of god. These are difficult conversations unless you know your own point of view and try to understand other people's points of view.

Art Intro

MY MOTHER FIRST DEVELOPED MY INTEREST IN painting and sculpture though her own interests and practices. These beginnings flourished in high school years, and I was especially motivated by an art teacher who was somewhat popular in Maine. He encouraged me to experiment, to follow the painting's guidance as it developed. I did paint and sculpt realistically but mostly pursued ideas of abstraction and construction. Color was important, as was contrast, uses and perceptions of space, direction, movement, music, rhythm, and emotion.

After high school, I lost the opportunity to access a studio easily, and, more importantly, was pressured by the academic demands of a liberal education at a leading university. After college, two years in the army, marriage, and thoughts of family, I needed to "go to work." No more art…less dreaming. But after about 44 years divided equally between two career paths, advertising/marketing and community banking, I retired and decided to pursue my art interest. Although I had not actually painted during my business career, my wife, Irene, and I had devoted some time to collecting fine art. In early retirement, I attended a very good art school to jump-start my reentry. Interestingly, after a few years concentrating on realism, I one day popped back into my interest in abstraction. The painting of ideas. I have included a few examples to relieve any tedium in my written words and to allow the visual to comment on the narrative.

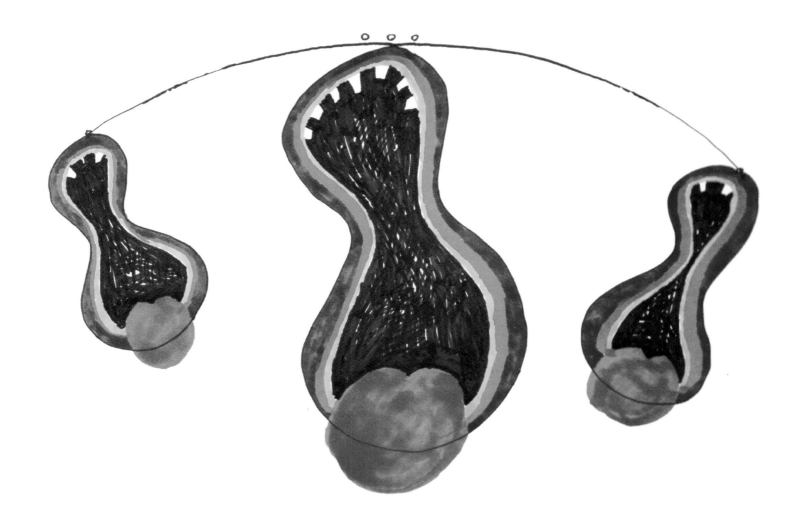

The Individual; the Group

THE GREATEST DEVELOPMENT IN POLITICAL THOUGHT was the opinion that the individual was more important than the group. That was one of the great debates and conclusions that formed the American Constitution and the Enlightenment in Western Europe. Today's American has a lot of affinity for groupthink and has trouble assigning individual accountabilities and responsibilities. Groupthink also makes it difficult to resolve your own viewpoint. And God help the person who dares to judge. Committees try to avoid accountability and responsibility, perhaps to relieve any individual pain. Unfortunately, the maturation of a committee leads to its becoming a bureaucracy and to pursuing its own interests over the individual's. Bureaucracy becomes the essence of putting the brakes to productive decision making. Perhaps because the strenuous, arduous debates of the Constitution seem rarely taught in today's academic world, more and more people have become enamored of groupthink. And group action or inaction. Political correctness. Committee structure tends to be least valuable in governance situations, especially during challenges, and most helpful in free-form creative exploration.

◀ *Extremists*, Pen and ink on paper, 14"x12"

Religion

RELIGION HAS ALWAYS PERPLEXED ME. THE BELIEVERS, the faithful, the religious vs. the nonbelievers, may all be after the same goal. What, after all, is the essential point or hope of religious development? I have thought it is the pursuit of goodness. My problem is that most religious practice is competitive. Before Abraham, the quintessential monotheist, men "created" something like 35 bibles, which tells me that God's word is a lot of man's word. Even allowing that the excuse for bad behavior is God's will, to give man his will, lots of really bad things develop—killings, destruction, power, subjugation. "I'm right, you're wrong. You're a nonbeliever."

Most of the admonitions of the Ten Commandments are proffered in all the great religions. And all call for their God. If the ultimate objective were goodness, wouldn't it result in *non*-competition? Wouldn't it result in wholehearted agreement? Unless, of course, your goodness was more important than someone else's.

For Heaven's Sake ▶
Pen and ink on paper, 14"x12"

Women's Rights

WHEN MY FATHER DIED, I WAS SADDENED. WHEN MY mother died, I felt a deeper sense of loss. She had influenced me in a special way. She had given me understanding, an appreciation of art and its practice, a love of athletics, a love of cooking. On the other hand, I also think I inherited from her a set of learning disabilities—and with them the understanding that they were things to overcome.

Importantly, because of her I am amazed that in the year 2015 we continue to define and debate women's rights. Perhaps elsewhere in our world they might be debated, but in America? In religions? And too, we see all around us the disintegration of families. High divorce rates. Careless child raising. A separation of man from woman. This is male vs. female competition to the detriment of all, especially family formation. Basically, we very much need to respect both females and males more…just the way other animals do.

Isn't it quite amazing that even today women still have a disadvantaged place in religious practices? Seems plenty dumb to me. Research constantly points to women's contribution to advanced societies and social practices, business practices, and political practices. One has to ask what kind of leader protects the status quo. Among other things, why are women's rights not central to American foreign policy?

Purpose

EACH OF US PROBABLY CONTEMPLATES OUR PURPOSE in life. Why are we here, after all? And that demands a lot of thought. If you do not have a purpose, do you really know what to do tomorrow? When thinking about purpose, I come down to two aspects, which I believe, though different, need inclusion to lead a balanced life. The first aspect of purpose is to understand how it applies to you. The second is to understand how it applies to your relationships with other folks.

Why both? I believe you should work to develop yourself into the most capable person you reasonably can be. It is a process of becoming self-sufficient and honest. But the singular *you* is not enough for most people. Nor should it be. People should naturally want more, be it fame, wealth, power, or just acceptance. Deep down, though, most people want, and need, to migrate from the personal to the grand.

In a sense, it is the journey from *taking* in order to form a better you, to *giving* in order to form a better society. So purpose becomes a continuum to be analyzed and thought about in both aspects all of your life. You should never stop developing purpose, for yourself as well as in relation to others. The process is fundamental to developing your judgment and character over time.

Execution

THINKING, OBSERVING, ANALYZING, AND UNDERSTANDING certainly are necessary before taking action. They should occur continuously throughout your life, with or without much activity. But at some point the rubber has to hit the road! You really have to *do* something, sometime. This can be worrisome. But tension, worry, fear are good stimulators. Don't be afraid of them. And energy is good, too.

Most people who do not act do not do things because they are uncertain of the outcome. They do not know what the future holds. They cannot sufficiently assess the results of their decisions. To repeat, they do not like worry, tension, fear.

Looking back, I have concluded that two aspects of my education (remember, I could not read or write very well) were particularly important in helping me develop—or create—a better understanding and approach to the future. Math and art especially seemed to help me see the future. They both extended my thinking into the unknown, into the possible. Math built on the known to project and sometimes prove future outcomes. Art overcame a blank canvas and actually helped portray what before then did not exist. My thinking, both visually and non-visually, was forced to hypothesize, extend logic, weigh influences, in order to be more confident in creating a future. And being more confident in having a sense of what I should work toward was immeasurably important in figuring out how to get there. This process also simplified any list of what to do, now and tomorrow. Being all over the place, as an alternative, leads to a really tough life. And "seeing" more into the future certainly helps control risk and worry.

◀ *Relationships #I*, Pen and ink on paper, 12"x9"

Risk

MANY PEOPLE LIVE IN THE PAST, OR ARE RELUCTANT to act, because they are risk-adverse. As mentioned previously, they want to avoid the tension, fear, and worry associated with risk. The future. But learning to understand and appreciate risk is a great talent and can be learned at levels that give people a real leg up on life.

Repeating experiences to avoid risk will not help you much. One critical aspect of managing risk is rarely mentioned. It involves one's character. And one's character is very important in developing judgment. Most "successful" people make judgments and decisions despite the absence of directly applicable information. "It was just the right thing to do" and "it's just common sense" reflect the talent of falling back on your principles, on your personal values, on your character in the absence of information.

Being "politically correct" often connotes values outside of your own. It represents a birds-of-a-feather thought syndrome: what I did was OK because "they" also did it. This hogwash leads to Pied-Piper activities of egregious dimension. Without developing your own sense of character, your very own conscience, as opposed to a societal conscience, you may find it impossible to avoid the pitfalls of life. Your own.

Momentum

THINK ABOUT MOMENTUM IN YOUR LIFE. MOMENTUM connotes movement, progress, building on the past for a better future. Not treading water. Not repeating the same comfortable experiences. Adding to your life because you have used your experiences to figure out better ways. "We always do it this way." "Don't rock the boat." "Be a team player." "Slow down." Perhaps all of these advisories can be helpful at times. But watch out: don't let them interfere with your creative contributions. Think about this old saying: "Boy, is he lucky!" Perhaps by using momentum, that person created his own luck. In one current example, most unions and their members have sunk into a primary role of repetitive self-protection. Today, unions should adopt a primary role of retraining workers to add momentum to their future productivity, security, and job formation. Management, boards of directors, and workers all need to use their past skills and endeavors to build new, more productive talents and jobs. Too much defense of current roles weakens everyone's future.

Art and the Pursuit of Beauty

ART, FOR THE MOST PART, HAS BEEN REPRESEN-tational, allegorical, and religion-based. Artists generally wanted to please patrons, comment on life, and pursue meaning and beauty. These days, art representing psychosis is important, and I guess is seen as progressive and meaningful. Being different for its own sake, especially if the art has some shock value, is desirable. Big and bigger is desirable. Costly is really desirable. Technique trumps communication. "What does it mean?" is often heard. And I know art elitists who hold some contempt for the question.

Beauty has acquired a certain air of boredom. "Pretty picture" is almost a death knell. Further, the use of technology in the creation of art allows for interesting nonhuman expression, yet may leave viewers feeling remote. Regardless of whether the art is representational or abstract, I am in favor of returning to the centrality of beauty and its power to create emotion. That will improve life faster. Beauty simply lifts one's spirit. Creating beauty in the world should join goodness as one of the greatest aspirations of mankind. Just remember the individual! Beauty is in the eye of the beholder.

Jazz ▶
Acrylic on canvas
24"x18"

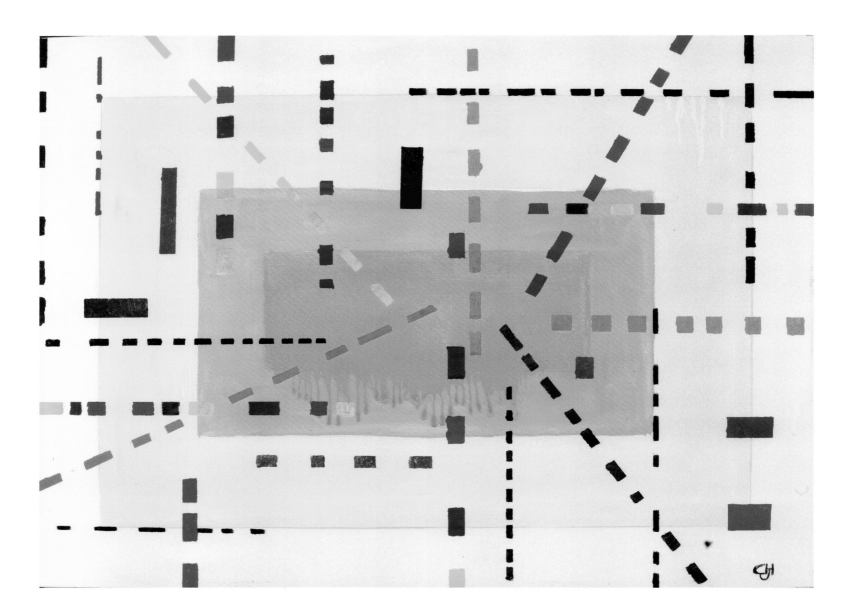

Art and the Pursuit of Freedom

STEPPING WAY BACK AND TRYING TO OBSERVE THE essential progression of art, it seems to have followed the essential progression of political man. That is, art has always been trending toward man's sense of freedom, releasing viewers from the strictures of the rational and realistic. Not being representational, abstraction relies unfettered on imagination and emotion. By removing real relationships, abstract imagery is freeing. It is a release that is its own object. Abstract art does not rely on representing natural objects; it represents its own original aesthetic. In many ways, this natural progression of art is the payoff of "thinking outside the box." Or how about *feeling* outside of the box? That's fun, too.

◀ *Urban #1*
Oil and acrylic on board
24"x18"

Space ▶
Oil and acrylic on board
12"x16"

Tension

RELAX. DON'T BE TENSE! YOU ARE UPTIGHT. EDGY. BOY, you are sensitive! Don't take all this so personally.

But you know, tension can be a real stimulator. It sharpens your thoughts, energizes, motivates, and influences others. For example, tension is a key concept in art development because visually and conceptually it helps wake you up. Tension demands a reaction. Attention. Some people get it. If you are not a little afraid from time to time, you are probably not adding to the value of your life. (Maybe you are lazy.)

And that problem, that blank page or white canvas, is pretty scary at times, isn't it? So work through it. Be a little more confident that you're OK. You are discovering. You could be learning. Do so every day.

Stop and Go ▶
Pen and ink on paper
12"x14"

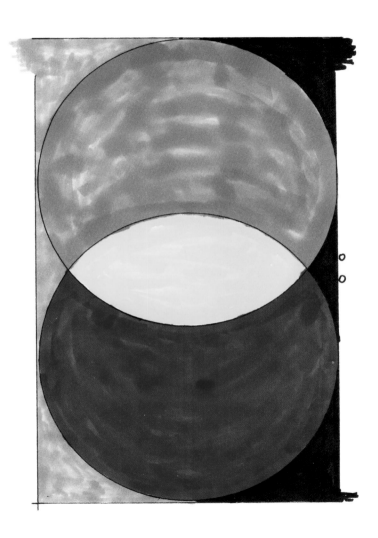

Balance

TENSION, NOW BALANCE? A CONUNDRUM. HAVE YOU ever noticed that people opine and vote for a balanced life? A balanced meal? Most people would be very satisfied with, and would vote for, contentment. They don't want to have to worry and seek balance. Don't rock the boat. Calm the waters. Don't stir things up. Relax.

How many people do you know who are always relaxed? Many (if not most) people don't really live that way. They need excitement, change, risk. They need stimulation. They need a fight! Rocking the boat is OK; it just needs a deep breath now and then. Art, for example, should create balance and tension for the purpose of aesthetic acceptability. Artists don't want your ear or eye wandering all over the place unless the art represents psychosis. I think we tend to wish for balance but naturally create tension. We all need both.

Fight

FIGHT IS THE MOST OVERUSED AND, TO ME, objectionable word in 2015 politics and media political reporting. Everybody seeks to curry favor by fighting more on *your* behalf than the competition's. But I don't want someone fighting on my behalf. I want them compromising and working for a better result for all. Fighting, after all, eliminates cooperation, understanding, and coordination. How do you get something done when people are self-righteous, "correct," and believe the end justifies the means—and fight?

"Do not compromise," they say. "Don't be a wimp." "Fight for what you believe in." Go back in American history about 250 years. The resolving of the Constitution was magnificent compromise. A value beyond what the world knew or appreciated. Nowadays, the brilliant intellectual and emotional architects of this effort are almost ignored. Make your educational institutions study this historical effort. Make the students of the world understand it. Yes, this was an American effort and very, very special. It was compromise, cooperation, and coordination at their best. American political extremes need to get with it. And we need to help the world get with it. It is a process we must improve and strengthen.

OK OK OK ▶
Pen and ink on paper
12"x9"

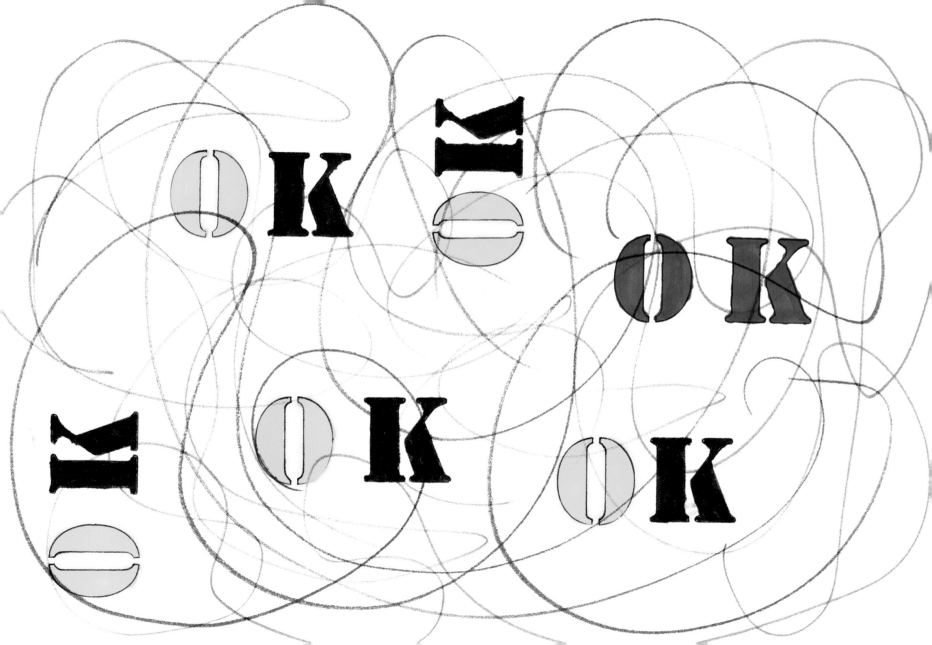

Truth and Fact

ASK SOMEONE TO DEFINE THE DIFFERENCE BETWEEN truth and fact. Ask someone if they are the same thing. To me, truth is what someone *believes* to be actual and noncontroversial. Fact, on the other hand, has nothing to do with belief. A fact is a fundamental element of existence. The difference between truth and fact has led to important institutions like our judicial system. Think about the importance of a jury. But don't just separate truth from fact at a courthouse. Do it in your daily life. You will have better discussions. A fact cannot be denied. A truth may be disagreeable, refuted, and even corrected. But you and your partner in the debate have to understand it is not a fact. Beliefs, truths, may change. Hopefully, we can all change for the better. Facts may only cease to exist.

Awareness

WE WERE ON A SMALL BOAT IN THE GALAPAGOS WITH six old friends for my wife's fiftieth birthday. At rare times, we needed to create our own fun. Once, after a wonderful dinner of just-caught clawless lobster, coleslaw, and orange cake with one candle, I invited everyone to play a game I had just heard of: create the biggest idea in the fewest words. No one was interested so I won. Here's my entry: "Patience takes time." Twenty-five years later, at a small dinner party, I repeated the invitation. One of our friends offered "awareness." That sounded pretty good. What do you think? How often has a lack of awareness caused misunderstanding, conflict, tragedy? Read more than one newspaper. Listen to more than one point of view. Don't stop your education at the boundaries of your neighborhood or when you get a diploma. Let the opposition speak! And listen!

◄ *Time*, Pen and ink on paper, 9"x12"

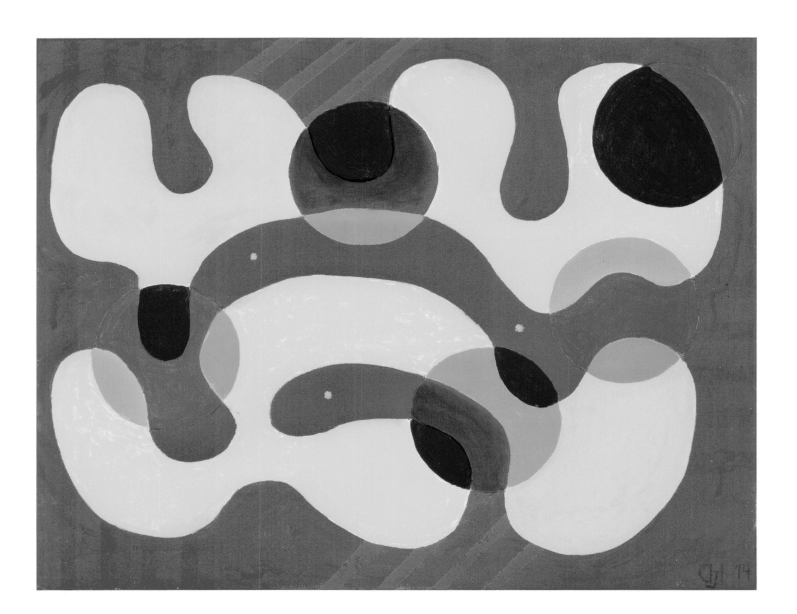

The Present

IN ANOTHER DINNER CONVERSATION, I INTRODUCED the idea that there is no "present." There are only past and future because "time waits for no man." The so-called present is in continuous motion. It moves constantly away from the past and through to the future. In terms of time, you cannot stop the present.

Think about this politically. Think about this in your personal relationships. Think about this as it relates to your truths. Think about this in relation to how you spend your time. Some good art attempts to stop time by being so realistic you are in the moment. But being in the moment is also a risk because it limits integration, transference, and expansion. It can be beautiful and, by definition, nostalgic…or desirable. Ditto for love.

◄   *Interaction*, Oil and acrylic on board, 20"x16"

Government

GOVERNMENT IS AN ETERNAL CONUNDRUM. HALF THE population of the world thinks government is inherently self-serving and half think of it as a force for goodness. The Enlightenment put it in its proper light. Government generally morphs from concepts of individual goodness to groupthink and promotion. To holding power. American founders knew this well enough.

The Achilles heel of all democracies is that once politicians are elected, they try to stay elected by catering to voters…they simply try to buy the vote. One way to aid this process is to weaken education so the voter does not appreciate critical or longer-term issues. Governments grow to dislike dealing in concepts of individualism because it is difficult. And at some point it becomes necessary to deal with groups. It is pragmatic and natural. This was key to our founders believing in a separation of powers and critical to protecting individual rights. To stay in power, politicians have been known to mislead and feed the self-serving motivations of voters. That is the bad side of human nature. Because of this almost inevitable moral weakness, term limits should have been addressed in the Constitution. But perhaps it's still not too late. Insist on term limits.

Trust Me ▶
Pen and ink on paper
12"x14"

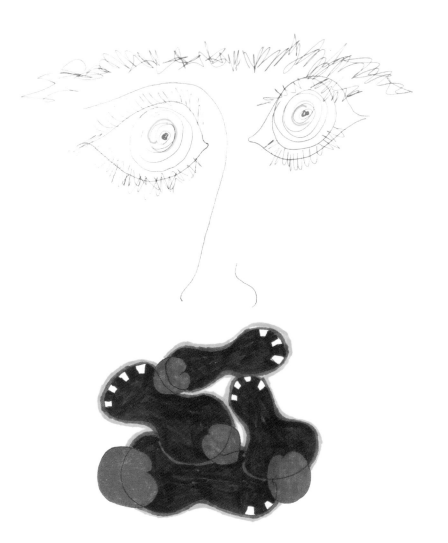

Government Math

GOVERNMENT MATH AND ACCOUNTING PRINCIPLES are a sham. Simply put, government should practice the same accounting principles as private enterprise. It does not. Why not? Over time, the government has learned to feed itself (bureaucracy) with rules permitting actions that *individuals* would not judge proper for themselves.

As for the math, here's a good one: "landslide" political victories nowadays require only 15–20% of the registered voters! The Bills—Clinton and de Blasio (NY mayor)—received less than 20% of the eligible voting public's votes, as did Barack Obama. And a lot of others. Obviously, 20% was enough because few citizens voted. If 40% of the available, qualified voting public does vote and the candidate receives 45% of this vote, that candidate has received 18% of all possible votes: 40% x 45% = 18%. This is now termed a landslide, a mandate. Go figure.

Group

BIRDS OF A FEATHER FLOCK TOGETHER. SO DO FISH, horses, and humans. Animals and people want to belong. Belonging is a great motivator in all things including religion. Part of this need is social; part of it is intellectual. We don't want to be wrong. If others agree with us, or we with them, aren't we less vulnerable, more correct, more righteous? More comfortable? More powerful?

Children learn this attitude early. "Johnny's parents don't make him do that…why should you make me do it?" Just because Johnny's parents are not correct in your eyes has nothing to do with the challenge. But it has a great deal to do with raising your children. It also has a great deal to do with reaching inside yourself and coming up with original creative activity. Being really *you*, not just part of your group or your neighbors' collective thought, is what honesty is all about. And following your conscience is a significant part of developing and being accountable for your sense of morality.

Relations #4 ▶
Oil and acrylic on board
36"x36"

Compromise

IS COMPROMISE WIMPY OR BRAVE? DOES COMPROMISE contain higher principles or lower? A criticism like "Don't you stand for anything?" is stinging. A compromise is often seen as giving up, losing the debate. The other side WON! After all, winning is everything. In a sports-crazed world, there is no second place.

But the Constitution disallows the one-winner syndrome in favor of allowing, in fact encouraging, lots of *individual* winners. Group interests, of course, reduce this opportunity in a major way. Anarchy vs. freedom… the halves? The growing efforts of extremist groups to limit Constitutional First and Fourth Amendment rights is a recent example.

◄ *Kick Ball*, Pen and ink on paper,14"x11"

Some 2014 commencement speakers had their right to free speech violated when groups successfully prevented their appearances. Sad. Dangerous. Stupid. Immature. Un-American. Yes, religion is still important.

Question

AN ANNOYING PRACTICE OF MINE IN DISCUSSIONS IS to keep asking questions until I feel I understand the core viewpoint of the other person. Annoying because most people have not really thought through their premise, reasoning, or conclusions and thus become frustrated with me for attempting clarity. For not understanding! This is especially true at cocktail parties.

And rather than stay at it, people often just resort to "OK, forget it." In many public schools, I have noticed that the inability to communicate, to understand, to appreciate words, is so acute that significant negative reactions are common. Mildly, it results in frustration. Severely, it results in violence.

If you cannot vent frustrations through speech or writing, you tend toward violence out of frustration. And we shouldn't be embarrassed by not knowing what a word means. Ask. Dig deeper. Same for ideas.

Interpretation

INTERPRETATION CAN BE VERY HELPFUL OR VERY misleading. Used by government folks, it is often very misleading…toward their own purposes. Media folks call it "spin." Interpretation used by good teachers can be very helpful to students who are seeking better expression, better understanding. If you don't understand someone, rather than interpreting their thoughts, tell them what you think they're trying to say and ask them if your paraphrasing is accurate. If not accurate, stay at it if it's important. If not important, move on to movie reviews.

Controversy ▶
Pen and ink on paper, 12"x14"

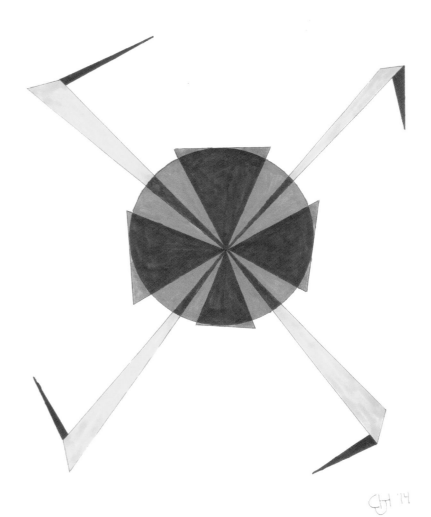

Intentions

GOOD INTENTIONS ARE SOMETIMES MORE problematic than helpful. Take the issue of escalating minimum wages, for example. In the short run, raising minimum wages will cause a loss in jobs. Many small businesses may not be able to afford the cost increase or be able to pass increased costs on to the consumer; they would ultimately have to reduce their staff. This is now a lively debate in the fast food industry. In the long run, such increases generally cause inflation as there is no gain in productivity. But to many, higher minimum wages are immediately gratifying—hence validating the choice. Forget the future and fundamental value.

Intentions also may go nowhere. "Well, I intended to do that," you might say. As though intentions in their own right are good enough. They are not. Remember: "With friends like that, who needs enemies?" If not executed, intentions are really just excuses. Think about setting objectives and goals instead.

Imagination ▶
Pen and ink on paper
12"x9"

Assumption

ONE OF THE MOST VALUABLE REALIZATIONS I experienced in the business world is very simple. What's in your head is rarely in someone else's when you need it to be. Therefore, I quickly learned not to assume anything. Some folks press the Send button on the computer for an important communication and think, "That's done." I advised everyone working with me that if they were trying to communicate anything important, they needed to follow up personally after the initial phone call or e-mail. Only as a last resort is it OK to *assume* someone thinks as you do…then with assumption, risk becomes huge. Hopefully, the assumption will be understood by and agreeable to all parties. Good luck.

Traffic

TO ME, THE TRUE GREATNESS OF ANY SOCIETY RESIDES in its ability to allow business, trade, value creation, and individual pursuit of happiness to flourish under law and order. Mistakes will certainly be made. But they will be more likely corrected at the street level than at the national level. Individuals connect and correct mistakes more quickly. Government bureaucracies are slow to respond and need the votes. Why is it that drivers can't go up a hill or take a curve without slowing and jamming traffic? My medical doctor father was fond of saying that most people only use half of their brain. Maybe that's an exaggeration, in traffic at least. Traffic becomes group activity. Traffic tends to be exacerbated by inefficient driving, lack of awareness, and righteousness. And these tend to be exacerbated by laziness. And these are the same things that affect government, leading to extreme bureaucracies. Add one: lack of accountability. Unless there is an "accident."

◀ *Highway Music*, Oil and acrylic on board, 24"x36"

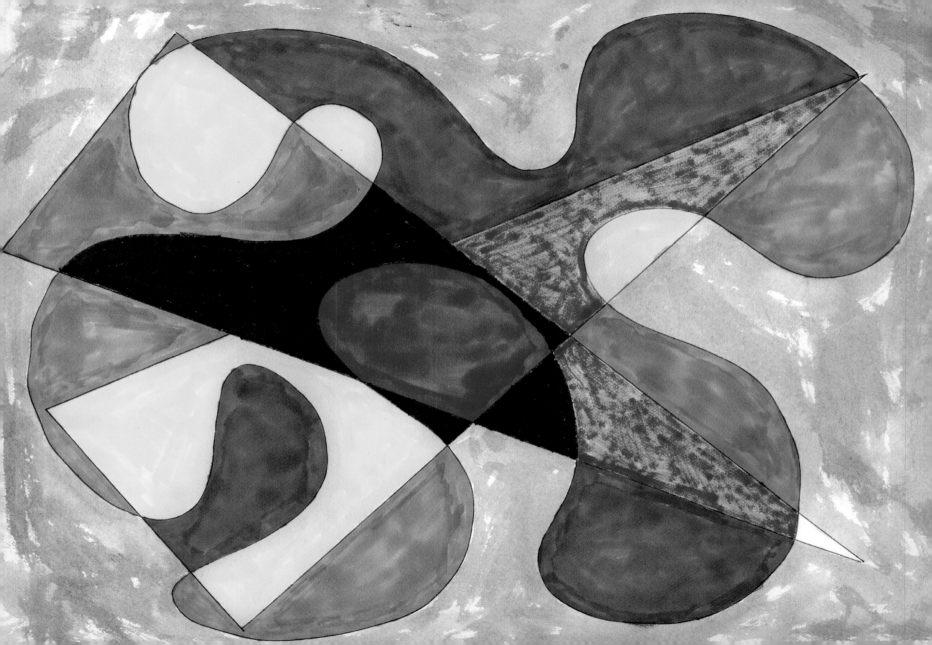

Money

MOST PEOPLE BELIEVE MONEY IS JUST A MEANS OF efficient trade and immediate gratification. But have you thought that it's also insurance? It may also create great differences in the kinds of influence one can bring to bear on their own future. How you think about your own money and enjoyment can create or destroy wealth. Monthly payment plans, debt, rent, and taking on risk are all ways to diminish your dollar if you are not very sophisticated. Government loves this stuff because it creates voter dependency. Witness student loans. Money is not only complex; it is at the center of most of our decisions, or should be. Beware when someone tells you "it's not about the money." What ever happens without the stuff? A little, I guess. Respect money. Do not respect its misuse. And continually think about what it really is.

◄ *Life*, Pen and ink on paper, 12"x9"

Lists

I MENTIONED THAT THERE IS NO PRESENT BECAUSE we move through time instantly and continuously. It is always gone and can never come back. So think about time. Think about how you spend it, waste it, or use it. Think about how much energy it deserves. Think about priorities. To-do lists.

Before I left the office every Friday, I made a Monday to-do list. The important stuff on top…even if I disliked the prospect of an item. I reviewed the list first thing every Monday—weighing whether the order needed to change. I started with item #1 and kept it on the list until completed. If stymied or prevented on one item, I moved on but always came back to the postponed task. Every day the list was updated for the next business day. Not liking to do something was not allowed to influence the list. This little exercise made time management far more productive. I actually worried less and did more. This is a common advisory but most people do not heed it.

Gratification

WE ALL NEED A LITTLE GRATIFICATION IN OUR LIVES. "For me" is OK in some measure. A tidbit of indulgence. That piece of chocolate? What harm could a little cake do? How about eggs and bacon for breakfast? Red meat? A little cheating here and there? Oh no; maybe that's going a bit far. Obesity has become a problem in our society. Again, our elected officials think they should take on this problem. We have been told red meat, animal fat, eggs, on and on, are bad for you. But we kept on eating them because we who love them really knew better, didn't we? We knew something so delicious should only be enjoyed in moderation. Years and years later, the government seems to have concluded that in moderation these things could be *good* things! We knew this all the time, didn't we? Our little gratifications have been OK, haven't they? Maybe these indulgences satisfied us quicker so we ate less in the long run. Who knows? I bet we are happier, though. Just don't forget the scale and mirror.

Non sibi

NOT FOR ONESELF? NOBLE? ULTIMATE KINDNESS? Generosity is good at all costs? On that theme or that rationale, let's redistribute wealth and make 90% of all populations happy. Flies in the face of enlightenment, doesn't it?

My brother, when we were around 11 or 12 years old, accused me one night of being out for only myself. At the time, that really hit me negatively. I thought I was a pretty good guy but had to do a lot for myself to overcome disabilities…to create a person who actually had something to give others.

I always believed that sympathy without strength, judgment, or your own accountability was a shallow pond. Even airplane crews issue a directive to put on your own oxygen mask before helping others. Yes, the sum of your life importantly includes helping others. Do a better job of this by making yourself better every day.

Ego

EGOTISTICAL…ALL FOR ME AND I DESERVE IT. DO IT my way. I am always right. A good friend came up behind me as I was cooking dinner for a small party and told me, "You're the only person I know who doesn't have an ego." I was surprised by that out-of-the-blue statement but assured him that I did. How could anyone get along without one?

Perhaps he really meant that I did not wear my ego on my sleeve. It has always seemed for me that the more it showed, the more unpleasant it appeared. And I always wanted to be liked, admired, respected, successful, rich enough (?), sexy—you get the picture.

To aspire is really good. To want things to improve, to be satisfying, to be helpful is wonderful. To want nothing or want for nothing is not what life is all about. So exercise your ego. It's fun. But don't overdo it. Remember balance in all things. And don't show your ego when your associate is not up to par. (I just took up golf. It gives a whole new meaning to the word *par*.) And ego helps back up confidence. How about a touch of pride?

◀ *The Beginning*, Acrylic on canvas, 18"x24"

Race

I DON'T MEAN RUNNING OR COMPETING…OR DO I? (Al Sharpton, are you still out there?) In 2015, I just had to take this on! If you want to be truly nonprejudicial, put race way down at the bottom on your list of what's important. More important are education, religion, family, friends, tribe, good (and less) government.

But race comes up a lot these days because its platform has bolstered the careers of a lot of lousy leaders. If you don't educate folks, you can tell them that nothing is their fault. You can tell them it's only their race that others use to blame for their lack of accomplishment. But how outdated are these false leaders? How could Obama have been elected president of the United States (twice!) if racial prejudice were so prevalent? White folks were largely responsible for his election…they, too, wanted hope and change. And they voted for him partly because he is black. Is that racist? Then, when he is called an incompetent executive by the same people who voted for him, some leaders call these accusers racist.

There are truly great black and Hispanic leaders, educators, business executives, lawyers, judges, athletes—Martin Luther King, Jr., Thomas Sowell, Oprah Winfrey, Marco Rubio. We need to listen to them more! Obviously, leaders need followers. Be a good, informed follower. Hold leaders accountable and know why. You may have to be courageous.

Traffic ▶
Pen and ink on paper
9"x12"

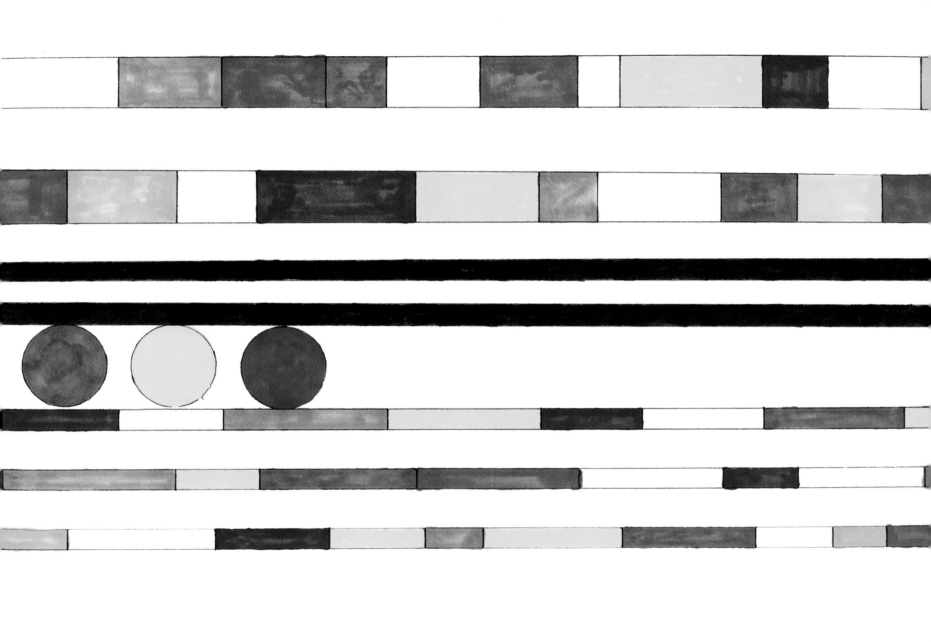

White

WHITE IS GENERALLY MISTAKEN FOR A COLOR. IT IS actually the combination of all color. Must mean something. Of course, an artist might remind you that rarely is white a pure and useful concept.

It is easy to make the mistake of using *white* (and *black*) generically in the political arena. It is also boneheaded. And it's important to consider this, as well, when talking about Muslims. After hundreds of thousands of white Americans lost their lives in their tragic civil war, one might ponder a Gettysburg for moving freedom forward, for everyone. For helping to open opportunity. Equal treatment under law and order. Thanksgiving.

Recognizing truth and accountability makes it a little harder to use excuses. Laying on the guilt might eventually weaken as a political motive. God help the left and right extremists. Maybe we all should be gray. Let's just be educated.

Black

BLACK IS NOT A COLOR, EITHER! BLACK AS A POLITICAL force is also losing potency as civil rights movements and opportunity become more apparent. New opportunities have threatened political arguments based on race. Perhaps to counter new opportunities, teachers' unions have taken over education from parents, teachers, and students, resulting in the dumbing down of our youth. If you are uneducated, if you cannot read or write very well (I know), you are vulnerable to being influenced by hogwash. Race is not as powerful as being uneducated. And whining about fairness belittles the wonderful accomplishments of our minority citizens.

People like to complain rather than express satisfaction. Not knowing things, not being educated morally or intellectually (white or black), lets you off the hook. No real decisions. People are and deserve better than this. Get rid of fraudulent leaders; know who they are. They're the ones who tell you your troubles are not your fault. It's black vs. white out there. Hogwash. I love being around *all* people, any person who wants a better character, who wants to develop his or her judgment, who wants to help others, who wants to give, who wants to create value.

Socialism

THE MEEK SHALL INHERIT THE EARTH. AMERICAN democracy hasn't lasted yet—it's only 250 years old—because through our history, groups rise and override individual freedoms. Politicians use a winning 20% of possible voters to claim "landslide" and "mandate" because no one understands simple math, including the media. And having a mandate means they can "do it their way" instead of bringing along all (or most) of the individuals who did or did not vote for them.

Those who believe that government can make most economic decisions and activities better than private enterprise are those who believe in socialism. Presidential economics in 2015 is pushing for redistribution of wealth. You didn't make that product, the government did. You can't replace lousy workers. The president says budget escalation and debt are rational, therefore inevitable after all. *(Cutting debt and spending is never "rational." Ask any politician or* most people and they'll say it's impossible to cut debt.)

As a business executive, I tried to use cost-control discussions first in an effort to improve productivity. But most of my executives had in mind good reasons to escalate or hold excessive spending levels. Eventually, I relied on what were perceived as arbitrary decisions to force debt and spending reductions in areas I deemed it necessary. That's what executives are paid to do and it's why most people don't want to be executives. And why their high pay is usually justified. Socialism has never worked except in societies whose citizens don't have to work much…countries with small populations and large natural resources. But socialism appeals to a warped sense of fairness. The old so-called joke: Two neighbors—one has a goat, one does not. The socialist planner creates equality: he kills the goat. Some joke!

◄   *Be Cause*, Pen and ink on paper, 12"x9"

Taking

ONE REASON I FEEL THAT RELIGION IS VERY IMPORTANT is that I have never experienced, or heard of anyone praying, to take something from somebody, to redistribute wealth from one person to another. "To give" is the message of religion. Do extremists agree with this?

Governments have to have the economic means to function. So governments begin by taking. It's called taxation. But the founding fathers of America knew that the power to tax could be very dangerous and could be easily abused. Now there are people who believe it is OK to take away more than half of what a person makes. We now see the government taxing authority abusing power and privacy for political ends. To take away from productive pursuits and give to nonproductive pursuits is to destroy value and humanism. To use the taxing authority to invade citizens' privacy is criminal.

The government should build bridges for effective commerce and development, but not bridges to nowhere. And acknowledging the inherent, inevitable bureaucracy of government, "too big to fail" is a foolish concept and a threshold concept to socialism.

Untitled #4 ▶
Oil on canvas
16"x20"

Judgment

WHEN HIRED FOR MY LAST JOB, I WAS TOLD THAT I WAS being hired essentially for my judgment. Not my related experience, which was minimal. Not my pertinent knowledge, also minimal. It was made clear that if the board found my judgment faulty, I would not last long.

Judgment is highly transferable to diverse circumstances, economic challenges, and the formation of your own character. We all know good judgment is not given us at birth. We have to learn to understand what it is and how we can mature it, grow it, and use it. Just plain old thinking, constantly, is very helpful in this process. Think more about yourself…critically; understand *you* without excuses. Know the difference between truth and fact. Prioritize. Everything in life has a difference in value. Try to figure it out. And remember: your good intentions are probably not enough.

Jest

A JESTER, AMONG OTHER THINGS, IS A PROFESSIONAL fool. Think of a court jester. In medieval times, rulers needed their court jesters, who were smart characters who knew the value of humor, self-deprecation, and good advice. They were also apolitical. Deep down, leaders risk becoming isolated. A jester can help bring them back to reality. And most of us find some charm or honesty in people not afraid to play the fool from time to time.

It never ceases to amaze me how powerful humor is in our relationships. If you rise to anger occasionally, remind yourself that you are about to alienate someone. Learn to play the fool. Didn't Ol' Blue Eyes have the right idea? "Where are the clowns? Send in the clowns."*

* From the musical, *A Little Night Music*, by Stephen Sondheim.

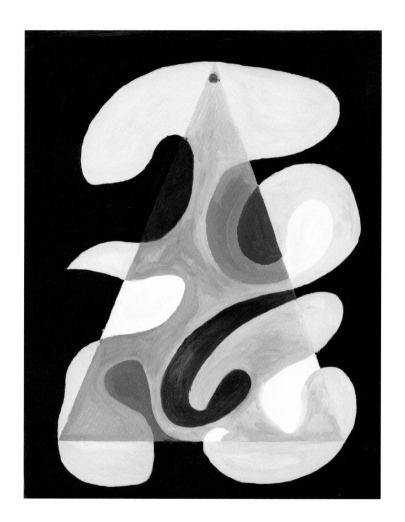

54

The Three C's

CONTROVERSY, COMPROMISE, COORDINATION. THESE three little words are the path to peace and prosperity. Memorize them. Should be the operating principle for all politicians.

I know I refer a lot to America's founding fathers, constitutionally speaking. But their efforts and interactions are among the greatest human accomplishments in the face of intellectual disagreement. Their attitudes, character, and dedication to high principles make modern politicians look sick.

The extremists—left, right, green, religious, no matter which gender—are immature, self-serving outsiders who cannot appreciate or judge the big issues. They have been dumbed down. Controversy is inevitable, and hopefully always will be. It is the gigantic importance of compromise and then coordination that needs understanding and dedication. For the greater good. For individual freedom. For less government and more personal responsibility. For more meaningful compassion. Things do need to get done. Stopping at controversy in order to win (or lose) is not generally a path to productivity and inclusion.

◀ *Black Peanuts*, Oil on board, 11½"x16"

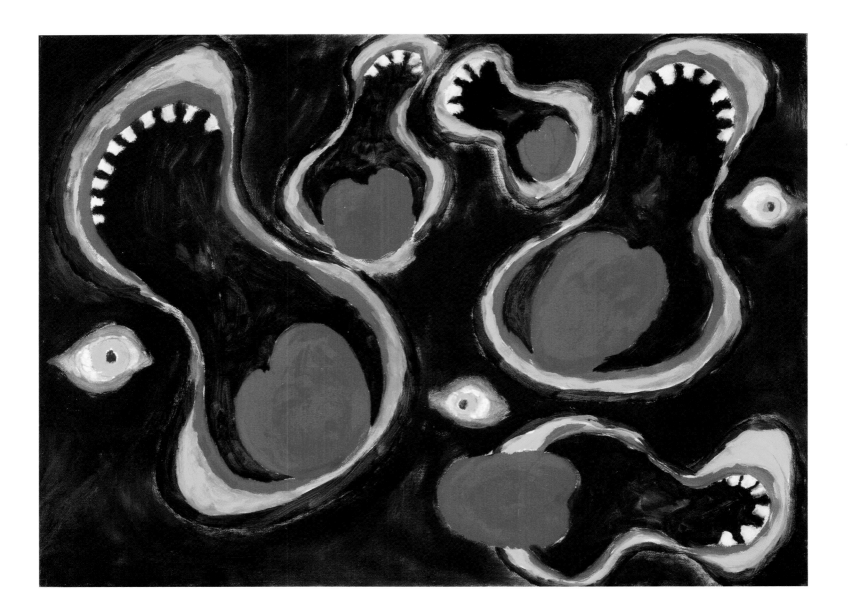

Politics

POLITICS IS A MATTER OF GETTING VOTES. WORTH-while leadership, on the other hand, is the art of creating broad human and economic value.

People tend to vote for what benefits them in the short run. Politicians try to give people what they want to satisfy their *own* aspirations. This pretty much guarantees the destruction of needed moral and economic values. So far, the Constitution of the United States has not prevented this wormy, natural tendency. American leadership began by establishing the greatest historic possibility for lasting moral and economic values yet achieved by any society. Today, political leadership is systematically destroying what was then begun. Weakening education, creating unmanageable debt, cheating, defrauding, hiding, lying, and pitting citizen against citizen are obvious techniques. This is sickening and severe. The takers are winning and destroying by gaining more votes. Now 50% of the U.S. population cannot judge or reason well because they are significantly under educated. Food stamp usage has grown by 50% in just a few years. Is this a new method of keeping people down? And after 100% mortgage products, at the government's insistence, we also have the student loan (government) program. We are now in a short five-year cycle of history repeating itself…the sins of the past.

◀ *Politics*, Oil on board, 24"x18"

Signs

AS I DO, DO YOU THINK THAT MOST SIGNAGE conditions broader thought? I do not mean ownership signage like "Mom and Pop's Deli," for instance.

Have you thought about these signs: No Loitering; No Spitting; No Dogs; No Cats; No Carts; No Speeding; No Dumping; No Littering; No Noise; No Food; No Drinks; No Running; No Walking; No Driving; No Watering; No Hunting; No Talking; No Trespassing; No Fires; No Camping; No Stopping; No Climbing; No Swimming; No Cars; No Bikes; No Trucks….What do all these have in common? "No." That will give you some idea of what government is about. REGULATION. Not about the positive, but the negative.

The essential activity of today's government is negative, which results in inadequate economic development. Just measure the quantity of written regulations in new business formation. The more regulation, the less chance a business—or a life—has to succeed. More government, fewer productive jobs. We know it…well, some of us should know it. And no "yes, buts."

Regulation ▶
Pen and ink on paper
14"x12"

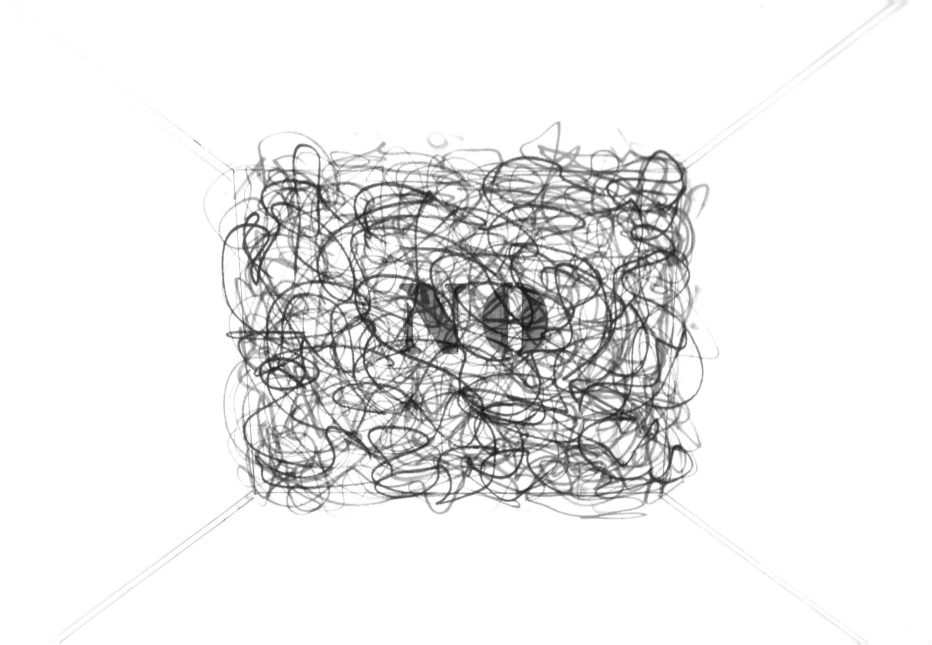

Trust (I)

WHEN YOU GET RIGHT DOWN TO IT, THE WORLD operates on trust. This goes against current lawyering interests, what most lawyers tell you. Lawyers, law, and regulations build vast bureaucracies, which mutate into pursuing their own interests, agendas, and benefits. Not yours.

In business, an executive gets few chances to violate the trust others place in her or him. In government, trust is violated all the time with increasing impunity. Maybe that is why our founding fathers made of point of stating, "In God We Trust." Trustworthiness is a cornerstone of one's character. It is about honesty, accountability, and reliability. Trust is better than any contract ever written. When trust is lost in trade, business, or medicine, most times the leader is lost. Not so with government-controlled associations, be they big banks, big unions, big agencies. Our society needs to work on this. And remember, chances are you cannot trust the contract! It looks as though we cannot trust the government, either.

Trust (II)

YOUR NEW FRIEND (OR OLD) LOOKS YOU SQUARE IN the eye and say, "Trust me." Uh-oh! Now you begin to get really worried. If real trust existed between the two of you, the words would not be needed. But real trust takes time to develop and may never develop. And trust can be lost in an instant. Don't be afraid of it; just be very careful, and never be made to feel guilty over it. Lend money to a friend or relative? Think of it as a gift, not a loan, and you will be better off. Don't trust the contract.

Leadership

TOUGH SUBJECT. WHAT'S YOUR DEFINITION OF leadership? Can be good or bad…effective or not. Most people assume that anyone in a leadership position is a leader. Unfortunately. My definition is that a leader causes things to happen that would not happen without him or her. Good or bad. But we all prefer good. Leaders (good) are supposed to accomplish things that ordinary folks cannot accomplish on their own. Leaders should have a sense of the future beyond that of ordinary people and their everyday desires. Leaders should recognize the merits, values, and aspirations of all the people in their care. And they must be great educators and communicators. Leadership positions have always been vulnerable to self-dealing, corruption, and power accumulation. However, I do not believe these enticements/faults should excuse bad behavior. I believe that laws governing punishments for bad behavior should call for punishments twice as severe for leaders as for ordinary folks. After all, we will have given them our trust and they have usually promised betterment. Leaders need to be held to a higher standard, or they should not be in leadership positions.

Attitude

SO, HOW MANY TIMES HAVE YOU HEARD THAT LIFE IS all about attitude? I am one of those who believe it is, most importantly, attitude that helps or hinders us through life.

My father advised me at a young age to say "Just great" or "Fine, thanks" when asked "How are you?" No matter how you are! He was sure most people didn't care anyway…unless the question was used as an opening for them to tell you how miserable *they* were. Indulgence, revenge, prejudice, depression…all bad stuff. Some of these negatives are related to chemical imbalances and other medical challenges. Many are not. Most people feel sorry for themselves occasionally. But to the extent your attitude is sour, you will be sour. And except for lemons and cherries, most of us don't like sour. Negative attitudes not only don't make friends or admirers, they handicap your own potential. I don't know one entrepreneur who thinks negatively.

I have watched a friend for 78 years live with a basically negative attitude—something was always wrong somewhere. Exhausting. Helps to develop a bad self-image and unhappiness. Train yourself to look at the good, the positive, and you should feel a little better about everything. Especially your weight.

Attitude ▶
Pen and ink on paper
14"x12"

63

Time

What really is time?
There is no present.
Time has a past
And time has a future.

Time has no present
For time never stops.
Time flows.
Time continues.
Time never stops.

You occupy time.
It flows through you.
But if you are in time past,
You are simply gone.
You cannot regain.

You can commit to the alternative,
The future, if even for a moment
(or continuously)
You can create.

You can become.

◄ *Get On With It*, Oil and acrylic on board, 24"x18"

Conclusion:

THINK ABOUT IT.

Fuzzy thinking helps no one.
Misrepresentation is immoral.
Goodness is creation.

So are you.

Be honest.

Lazy is a crime against humanity.
Taking is a crime against humanity.

Mind is reason. Develop it.
Tongue is expression. Practice.
Eyes are seeing. Look.
Heart is feeling. Use it.
Heart trumps all.

Know yourself.